32 Career Enemies

Table of Contents

Introduction 2

Enemy #1: How You Can Negatively Affect Your Own Career..........4

Enemy #2: How Your Family Can Affect Your Career........................6

Enemy #3: How Your Friends Can Affect Your Career 8

Enemy #4: How Your Location Can Affect Your Career 10

Enemy #5: How a Lack of Education Can Affect Your Career.........12

Enemy #6: How Your Attitude Can Affect Your Career....................14

Enemy #7: How a Bad Appearance Can Affect Your Career...........16

Enemy #8: How Laziness Can Affect Your Career 18

Enemy #9: How Procrastination Can be an Enemy to Your Career20

Enemy #10: How Not Being Dependable Can Affect Your Career..22

Enemy #11: How Not Willing to Work Your Way up The Ladder Can Affect Your Career 24

Enemy #12: How Not Being Prepared Can Affect Your Career.......26

Enemy #13: How Not Being Organized Can Affect Your Career.....28

Enemy #14: How Your Competition Can Affect Your Career...........30

Enemy #15: How Your Boss Can Affect Your Career 32

Enemy #16: How Your Organization Can Affect Your Career.........34

Enemy #17: How Insubordination Can Affect Your Career 36

Enemy #18: How Office Politics Can Affect Your Career.................38

Enemy #19: How Not Getting Along With Co-Workers Can Affect Your Career..40

32 Career Enemies

Enemy #20: How Poor Work Performance Can Affect Your Career 42

Enemy #21: How Being a Workaholic Can Affect Your Career 44

Enemy #22: How too much Pride Can Negatively Affect Your Career 46

Enemy #23: How Being Resistant to Change Can Affect Your Career 48

Enemy #24: How Not Being Appreciative/Grateful Can Affect Your Career 50

Enemy #25: How Unemployment Can Affect Your Career..............52

Enemy #26: How Not Staying Up to Date Can Affect Your Career .54

Enemy #27: How Your Social Media Activities Can Affect Your Career 56

Enemy #28: How Your Health and Fitness Can Affect Your Career 58

Enemy #29: How Choosing the Wrong Career Can Affect Your Career 60

Enemy #30: How Your Personal Live Can Affect Your Career........62

Enemy #31: How Using Alcohol and Drugs Can Negatively Affect Your Career...64

Enemy #32: How Criminal Activities Can Affect Your Career 66

About the Author 68

32 Career Enemies

Introduction

During the course of your career, there will be several enemies that you must face. Some of these enemies will come when you least expect them. In order to defeat or control your career enemies, you must be able to recognize your enemies and establish a plan to deal with them.

A career enemy will not always be a co-worker (as you will learn in this book) but instead it could be your life style, medical condition, or your location. By being aware of the many challenges you can experience alone your career path, you will be able to unlock your true potential to constantly advance.

I would recommend that you print a copy of this book and use the extra space at the end of each chapter to keep notes. This book will provide some highlights to assist you alone your career journey.

32 Career Enemies

Enemy #1: How You Can Negatively Affect Your Own Career

Although you may be an extremely driven, ambitious individual, you can sabotage your own career. If you do not take care of yourself, you can ruin your chances of a promotion or entrance into the career field of your choice. Self-discipline is the key to advancing your career, but this does not necessarily mean self-discipline to accomplishing all your work by the deadline or staying late at the office.

First, consider your stress level. Your job may be extremely stressful, and your life outside of work may be stressful as well. It is a well-known fact that people who are stressed do not sleep well, are more susceptible to illness, and that they do not function as well as they might at their work. If you are over-worked, it is vital that you take time out to rest. Vacation, reading some of your favorite book every night, going for a walk, exercising, and being with friends and family are some positive ways to counter your stress level.

Next, think about how hard you work. If you are too stressed to do your job well, you may just be shooting yourself in the foot even by showing up to work. Others will notice that you work too much, that your performance is slipping, and they may move in to get the promotion that you have been working too hard to earn for the last year.

Finally, prioritize your life. When you prioritize what is most

32 Career Enemies

important to you in life, you may find that your career isn't all that you thought that it was. This means that you may find more pleasure in your family and hobbies than in your work. This, in turn, can make your more relaxed and better able to do your work. Your quality of work may increase, and you might just earn that promotion you've been seeking.

Working hard is important, but working too hard can land your career in the gutter. Your health, personal and professional relationships, and your career will likely suffer if you take your work and your life too seriously. Discipline yourself to lighten up, and just do the best you can without going overboard.

32 Career Enemies

Family supports each other. At least, that is how it is supposed to be. In a perfect world, your family members would understand your chosen career path and would do whatever they could to ensure your success. However, this is not always the case. At times, you may have to take a stand against your family to pursue your chosen career path.

1.) You Can't Do That – This is a common sentence family members -- especially parents – like to tell young members, and older ones, about the careers they want. Parents won't pay for students to study music. Spouses tell each other they are too old to go back to school to train for another career. Be ready to respectfully combat this sentence if your family tries to say it to you. Have a plan to counter their arguments, such as knowing what scholarship opportunities are available.

2.) You Spend Too Much Time at Work – This is a tricky one. While you must work hard to earn a promotion or get an award at work, you must balance your priorities. Make sure your family is on board with your working more hours for a time so you can get a promotion and salary increase. Make time on the weekends or early in the morning to be with your kids. Don't neglect your family, and avoid making your career your entire life for long periods of time.

3.) You Don't Know What You're Doing –Unwanted advice is one of the most annoying contributions family members may make to your career. You can respond with, "I appreciate your

32 Career Enemies

suggestions. However, I believe that my choice is the best one." Be respectful as you respond to them, but stand firm in your decisions, too.

Family members have a stake in your career to an extent because their lives are affected by the choices you make in some respects. However, it is up to you to decide the direction you want to take your career. Know what you want, how you plan to get there, maintain respect for family members, and you will be well on your way to the career you want.

32 Career Enemies

You should have a social life outside of work. That is a given. You should have friends at work, too. Otherwise your days in the cubicle would be even more monotonous. However, it is essential to be aware of the ways that your friends can negatively affect your career. When you know what to look out for, you can discipline yourself to stay on track.

1.) Distraction on the Job – While it's fine to have a chat during the day with your friend, spending twenty minutes in the break room when it's not break time, talking about topics that have nothing to do with work is a waste of your and your company's time. Also, avoid answering incoming texts, posting to social media, sending personal emails, or being on the phone with friends during the day.

2.) Social Media – Those dreaded pictures that your friend took at the bar last night when you were out last night - They made it onto your friend's social media page, and you were tagged in the photo. If you are looking for a job, had a great first interview, but then the potential employer sees you online carousing with your friends, there's a good chance you won't get the job. Don't kid yourself that employers don't look at social networking pages of current and potential employees. They do.

3.) Bad Advice – Your friends may give good advice most of the time. Take what your friends say about your career path

32 Career Enemies

with a grain of salt, however. If you have an annoying boss, avoid acting on your friend's advice to load a virus on his computer or make negative comments about her online. Your friends will naturally take your side in a conflict you have at work. Try to remain objective, and think about the long-term before you make any rash decisions based off their suggestions.

Friends make the workplace and time outside of work enjoyable. Still, they can cause you to make errors that can cost you a new job or a promotion. Be careful what you say and do related to work. Stay focused on your career goals.

32 Career Enemies

Enemy #4: How Your Location Can Affect Your Career

Being in an area of your country with a large number of employers in your field is essential to getting a good start in, and advancing in, your career. If you choose to live away from where the action is, there is a good chance that you will not be considered among the up-and-coming professionals to hire when jobs open.

1.) The Boondocks Do Not Offer Jobs – When you look for a job in your profession, you probably won't find what you're looking for out of major urban and suburban areas. Now, this may not be the case if you want to work, say, on a ranch as a cattle driver or at a summer camp as a director. In that case, you may find just what you want in rural areas. Teachers who want a small-town environment in which to work may also prefer to work in smaller areas. However, if your degree is in international development, you should work in New York or Washington, D.C., which serve as the headquarters for major nonprofits. Nonprofits and governments offer positions in rural areas as well, but it's good to get your foot in the door in a larger city.

2.) The Pay is not as high. – Just for kicks, go check out the websites of a local, urban school district's teacher salary schedule. Then compare that with a more rural district a few miles away. In many cases, the rural areas – provided the

32 Career Enemies

property taxes are not as high – will offer significantly lower teacher salaries than urban areas. This is just one example of the fact that urban areas tend to pay more for the same type of services than rural communities.

3.) You'll Miss Out. – If you want to know what is going on in your industry, working in a large city is where to be. You will be among the first to hear of industry or company changes. You can better adjust your career plan by switching to a competitor or trying for a promotion. You will be more educated about your job and industry simply by living near the center of the action.

If you prefer rural life, and you can make ends meet on a lower salary, living away from the city is right for you. However, if you want to advance your career by knowing what is going on, live in the city, where salaries are higher, and more professionals like yourself work and live.

32 Career Enemies

Enemy #5: How a Lack of Education Can Affect Your Career

It is no secret that not having an education can hurt your wallet and bank account. Lack of schooling often simply translates into a lower paycheck than someone with a college degree. When you take a look at the hard numbers, however, the reality is more serious than most people imagine.

High School

The median annual income of a person aged 25 to 32 with a high school diploma in 2012 dollars was $28,000, according to a 2013 study published on PewSocialTrends.org. In the United States, that is barely a livable wage for a single person. Trying to raise a family on that amount without government assistance would be next to impossible. The share of this sub-section of society that lives in poverty was 21.8 percent. The news doesn't get any better when you look at the unemployment rate for the same group: 12.2 percent.

Two Years of College

Specialized training in vocations such as auto mechanics or nursing can lead to incomes that are as high as those of people with bachelor's degrees. These professions often require two years of college. The median annual income of individuals who have completed two years of college was $30,000, according to the same study. While the income does not significantly increase with a two-year degree in general,

32 Career Enemies

the unemployment rate drops 4.1 percent to 8.1 percent. The share of those living in poverty with two-year degrees was 14.7 percent.

Bachelor's or Higher

Four years or more in college increases a person's median annual income to $45,500. The percentage of those with at least a bachelor's degree in poverty was just 5.8 percent, and the unemployment rate was just 3.8 percent.

While these numbers certainly do not represent the fact that some people who enter apprenticeship programs, start their own businesses, who have a knack for finding profitable employment opportunities, or who quickly acquire the skills necessary to advance on the job earn as much or more than people who earn college degrees, these situations are not the norm. Earning a college degree is an essential first step to getting your foot in the door of the career you want.

32 Career Enemies

Enemy #6: How Your Attitude Can Affect Your Career

Negativity is the nail on the coffin for career advancement. A bad attitude can end any chance you have of getting the promotion you want. It can also cause your colleagues to hate being around you. You will lose out on potential friendships and special assignments by complaining and being pessimistic.

First, think about how you feel when you hear a friend complain every time you talk to her. No doubt you feel tired just being around her, and you don't want to pick up the phone when she calls. The same is true of the people with whom you work. If you constantly complain about your boss, gossip about others, or just complain that your head hurts for the fifth time in one day, you will find that fewer and fewer people want to be around you.

Second, as a natural result of people not wanting to be around you, you will be alone at lunch, left out of after-work dinner invitations, and generally alone at work. No one will stop by your desk for a chat or want to talk to you for more than a couple of moments. You miss out on supportive relationships at work and outside work by being negative.

Finally, a negative attitude will find its way to your boss. When the time comes to consider people for special assignments that lead to promotions, chances are that you will not be

32 Career Enemies

considered. If you are known for being curt and rude to customers, or you have a reputation for regularly sending negative criticism to subordinates instead of positive feedback at times, you will not garner your boss' favor. You may even cost your company profitable business and good employees who will not want to work with your company just because of you.

Phrase your words to be more positive. Consider the bright side of challenging situations. Make a phone call to an employee to say thank you for a job well done. Smile more. These small actions can make or break not only your professional and personal relationships, but also your future in your career. A few extra minutes of your time to be positive can make a world of difference.

32 Career Enemies

Enemy #7: How a Bad Appearance Can Affect Your Career

You may feel that it is a waste of time and effort to find a way to get rid of the wrinkles in your clothes before you go to work in the morning. Other people don't, though. While you don't have to care what other people think about your appearance to the point of spending hundreds of dollars and hours of your time trying to impress them, it is important to maintain a basic professional appearance on the job.

When you take the time to brush or comb your hair in the morning, you show your employer, colleagues, and customers that you care about what you look like. Appearances can be deceiving, yes, so wearing three layers of make-up and the latest fashions does not mean that you are any good at your job. Showing that you don't care what you look like at all, however, can harm your career.

1.) Customers will notice. No one really wants to do business with someone who didn't take a shower, brush his teeth, comb his hair, or who is wearing yesterday's clothes. Customers get the impression that you are unprofessional, and they will take their business elsewhere.

2.) Colleagues will notice. Being unkempt translates into people not really wanting to be around you. If you don't care about what you look like to a basic degree, they may not think that you would be the right person to have on their teams. You

32 Career Enemies

miss out on the chance to develop relationships with colleagues who are put off by your appearance as well.

3.) Employers will notice. What will the quality of your work be like if you can't even take care of yourself? Will you drive customers away or make colleagues wary to work with you? These are questions that will likely pop into an employer's mind when you apply for a job. If you are already working, and you start to let your appearance slip, employers may wonder if there is something going on at home that causes you to not care about your appearance. Their minds may then naturally wander to wondering how you are doing on the job.

32 Career Enemies

Enemy #8: How Laziness Can Affect Your Career

Working hard is the key to career advancement. Being lazy can stop your career in its tracks or even cause it to move backwards. Taking the initiative and being ambitious are what will get you in the corner office with the window. Laziness can cause others to think less of you, cause you to lose your job or miss out on a promotion, and lower the quality of your work.

First, laziness affects your relationships with your colleagues and boss. Working with you on a team will be a drag to colleagues who know that you turn out poor-quality work or that you don't turn it in at all. Maybe you're late meeting your deadlines because you're lazy, and you cause other people's work to suffer as a result. Your boss will notice if you are lazy as well. This can make him not want to support your career advancement.

Second, laziness can lead to your not being aware of what is new in your field. If you don't seek out training opportunities, go to conferences, and try new and innovative ideas in your job, you may be passed up by your colleagues on their way to better salaries and promotions. You may even lose your job if you are too lazy to learn anything new about it. When the list for lay-offs is made, your name will be at the top of the list.

Finally, the quality of your work suffers if you don't make follow-up phone calls to customers, proofread your emails before you send them, or don't practice giving a presentation beforehand. Your laziness leads to your getting a reputation

32 Career Enemies

as someone who does not care about her work. Customers won't want to work with you because your work is shoddy. Finding a new job if you get laid off or fired may be difficult because no one wants to write you a recommendation letter. They know you won't work hard in whatever new job you apply for.

Laziness snowballs into being fired and earning a bad reputation in your field. Work hard, and try your best to show your colleagues and customers what you can do. Working hard simply feels good as well. It will do wonders for your general sense of well-being.

Enemy #9: How Procrastination Can be an Enemy to Your Career

Waiting until the last minute to accomplish projects can be the death knell to your career. When you wait to finish a project, you take a significant professional risk. You may end up in a dead-end job and lose opportunities for advancement if you procrastinate. You also put your colleagues' work in jeopardy when you work on a team project.

First, procrastination negatively affects your team mates. If you are responsible for one part of a project, and you wait too late to finish it, your colleagues may not finish their work on time. This can turn them against you. You may find that they do not want to work with you. This can preclude you from being included on future teams. Some projects can lead to invitations to apply for higher-level jobs if you perform well. If you procrastinate, it can show your boss you don't care about your colleagues and that you aren't a team player.

Next, procrastination causes you to have to rush to finish your work too fast. When you rush, the quality of your work suffers. When that happens, it also indicates to your boss that you don't care about your work enough to do it well. You can imagine that if an opportunity for promotion comes up, you will likely not be on the list of potential candidates.

Finally, procrastination can push you into a job with no advancement opportunities. If you always wait until the last minute, you are the one that ends up losing out. Your opportunities to further yourself in your chosen career diminish significantly when you wait until the last minute.

In conclusion, procrastination leads to stress, which can also cause you to perform poorly on the job, increase tensions with your colleagues, and cause you to neglect other work assignments. Waiting also means that you may not have the resources you need at the last minute to finish the work well. Procrastinating is not the way to advance your career, so break up your projects into manageable tasks you finish at set deadlines well in advance of your final deadline in order to succeed.

32 Career Enemies

Enemy #10: How Not Being Dependable Can Affect Your Career

You showed up late for work again. Little do you know – and little may you care – that the co-worker you were to relieve now has to pay the babysitter another hour's worth of wages because you were late. Oh, and he doesn't get overtime pay to make up the cost. Not being dependable has ramifications beyond just you. It affects many others. The worst impact it has, however, is on your career.

1.) Not being dependable leads to a lack of trust. If your employers and colleagues cannot trust you to complete your work on time and in a high-quality manner, you can expect them to start excluding you from teams that work on assignments that lead to promotions, from being considered for new jobs, and from being considered a trustworthy person in general.

2.) No one will believe what you say. You may offer three dozen excuses in a month about why your report was late or why you broke yet another promise to someone at work, but no one is going to care. They think you cannot keep your word and that you lie to save yourself from getting in more trouble. Even if you do have legitimate problems that affect your work, it's better to be honest about them than to give pathetic excuses.

3.) You develop a bad reputation. Being thought of as a liar

32 Career Enemies

and someone who does not keep his word translates into your having a reputation as someone who is not good to work with or hire. You may find no one wanting to write your recommendation letters for new jobs. Companies in the same industry have a tight-knit human resources circle. Word travels fast about employee's characters and work ethic. You may face closed doors when you apply for a new job.

It is best to do what you are going to do, when, and how you say you are going to do it. Doing so gets you in good with employers and colleagues. You'll have a reputation as someone people can count on and trust. This is especially important during difficult times in an organization when everyone needs to go the extra mile to ensure success.

32 Career Enemies

Enemy #11: How Not Willing to Work Your Way up The Ladder Can Affect Your Career

Not having the drive to succeed in your chosen career path can both negatively and positively affect your future. Your level of interest in your current position will, in large part, determine your future professional stature and personal well-being. Carefully consider where you want to be career-wise before you decide that you are not willing to work your way up the career ladder. Make a list of the pros and cons to help you make your decision.

One way that not being career ambitious will benefit you is that your stress level is likely to stay much lower in your current position than if you seek a promotion. This can help you stay healthier in the long run. In addition, you will learn the ins and outs of your job better than anyone. You will be the expert in your position that others will go to for advice and training. Furthermore, you can seek horizontal movement in your company to gain new skills, and you can focus on perhaps starting a business of your own in which you are really interested. Finally, you won't have to compete with your co-workers for promotions, which can cause workplace tension.

On the other hand, not wanting to climb the career ladder can encourage the perception that you are lazy or not committed to your company or industry. It also can appear that you are not willing to learn new skills or to accept a challenge.

32 Career Enemies

Additionally, you risk burnout if you stay in a job that is not challenging and mundane. Finally, your paycheck will stay the same over the years. This can make it more difficult to save money and to invest it.

As you decide whether to apply for a promotion or a new position with a better job title at a different company, carefully examine the good aspects and the downsides of each choice. In the end, you are the one who must be comfortable with your decision. Avoid making your decision based on what others will think of you. Think of your health, your family, and your future goals.

32 Career Enemies

Enemy #12: How Not Being Prepared Can Affect Your Career

Say you have a training to conduct coming up in the next week. You don't prepare what you are going to say. You just know the basic topic and have a rough idea of the course's outline. You then walk into the training room and realize that you don't have the materials that you need and that you didn't think through how to do the lesson's activities very carefully.

If this is how you run your training, your students will notice. They will know you have messed the training up and that you are not prepared. You will not appear to be as in control as you should be. The flow of the training will be compromised. No one learns as much as they should from you, and word gets around that you are an unprepared and ineffective trainer.

Once word gets around that you are not very good at your job, you may not be allowed to do that training anymore. Students won't ask to have you teach them, and you may even be fired. You make the organization you work for look bad, and you don't do your career any favors by damaging your reputation each time you come to class unprepared.

Whether or not you train people for a living, being unprepared for your work reflects negatively on you. It is true in any profession that if you are not prepared, those around you can easily see it. They may think you are a procrastinator that doesn't care that much about his work to think it through

32 Career Enemies

carefully. They may also believe that you don't know your job as well as you should because you appear to bumble through presentations or your reports lack the necessary data or analysis to be useful to your boss or clients.

Think step-by-step through any task you have to do for work well before you have to have it done. Then work through each step in your mind or on paper to anticipate any difficulties, like not having enough materials. Being prepared for possible problems indicates that you stay one step ahead of problems and that you have considered how to solve them before they arise.

32 Career Enemies

Enemy #13: How Not Being Organized Can Affect Your Career

Organization is a sign of being prepared. It indicates that you have thought ahead of the game and that you are ready to solve problems that may come up. When an employee is organized, bosses and clients are confident in her to do her job well.

Disorganization, on the other hand, makes people nervous. Think back to when you were in college or high school. When a teacher fumbled through his papers looking for something, what was the atmosphere in the classroom like? It may have felt awkward, or the center of the activity in the room was with the students as they ignored the teacher.

Another example of the harm disorganization can cause is when your boss calls you up and asks for the latest sales numbers for the quarter. You may have input the figures into the database, but you haven't yet compiled and analyzed them. You should have had this done two days ago, but you forgot to email the manager of a particular region to get his sales numbers in beforehand because you didn't write it down in a to-do list. So your data is not only disaggregated, it is also incomplete. What is your boss going to think when you answer the phone?

You demonstrate that you are not on top of your game, that you are unprepared and scatter-brained. You cannot get your act together to handle important details like getting the data

32 Career Enemies

you need before your report is due. Your boss loses confidence in your ability to do your job well. The end result may well be that your boss starts looking for someone else to fill your shoes.

To avoid appearing disorganized, take time every day to clean off your desk before you leave and to create a prioritized to-do list for the next day. Make time in the morning to review that list and adjust tasks as necessary. Break down larger projects into smaller tasks with due dates well before the final project is due. File your papers away twice a week into their correct folders. Update your schedule book or online calendar every time you need to make a change. Taking small steps such as these will help you appear – and feel – as if you are in control of your job.

32 Career Enemies

Enemy #14: How Your Competition Can Affect Your Career

Competition comes in many forms. It could be that your company's competition affects your career. It could also be the case that someone in your office is considered to be your competition. No matter its origin, competition can spell disaster for your career if you do not know about it in advance. Be prepared to handle your competition by knowing what to expect from it ahead of time.

1.) Company Competition – Your company's competition may affect your career in a number of ways. For example, it may offer higher wages than your company can afford. It may set low standards for employee maintenance in the industry, resulting in your company dropping benefits or lowering wages.

2.) Outside Competition – Individuals on the outside of your company who want to be hired on at it can also affect your career. Younger workers with more and more recent college educations can take your job. They will also work for lower wages, pushing you into obsolescence. They force you to take stock of your job and to reevaluate whether you need to get some more credentials to remain relevant and on the cutting edge of your field.

3.) Inside Competition – Someone who wants your job or the promotion you've been wanting can also negatively affect your

32 Career Enemies

career. They may work harder, longer, and be more efficient than you for a time just so they look good to your superiors. This can be just the spur you need, however, to start working even harder in your current position. Avoid turning the situation into a down-and-dirty competition in which you say bad things about the other person or purposely try to sabotage her chances of getting the position she wants. Simply focus on improving yourself.

Competition can come from many corners. Be aware of your competition so that you can best plan a line of defense and attack to preserve your job and your chances of getting an even better one. Competition can be good in that it spurs you on to improve yourself, but it can also be negative if you ignore it or simply aren't aware that it even exists.

32 Career Enemies

Enemy #15: How Your Boss Can Affect Your Career

Bosses are ideally supportive and encouraging. They help you to access appropriate professional development. They train you in new responsibilities. They say, "Well done." This may all be true for some bosses. However, some bosses do not succeed in these areas of employee management. Instead, they may simply be road blocks on your way to a successful career.

First, bosses may not provide the professional training opportunities you need. If they are not up what is new in your industry, they may not be able to plug you in to the best trainings that will propel you forward in your career. They may be more worried about day-to-day problems of management instead of being focused on the long-term future of your career.

Additionally, bosses may simply not like you. If you have done something to upset them, they may take that personally and purposely stand in your way when you try to move up the career ladder. They may do this by refusing to give you a recommendation for a promotion or for a new job. They may favor another employee who is less qualified for a particular assignment. If you face this situation, remain respectful of your boss at all times. Avoid burning any bridges that you may need later.

Finally, some bosses do not offer much in the way of

32 Career Enemies

encouragement, either verbally or in writing. This can be a bit demoralizing, and it can, in fact, keep you in the dark about whether you are doing your job well. While you don't want to look as if you are fishing for compliments, you can ask your boss if there is room for improvement in your work. This indicates that you are trying to do your best.

If you are faced with a boss who does not have your best interests for your career at heart, you will have to be more diligent than usual in advancing your own career. Seek out your own training opportunities, remain respectful, and find out what you can do to well on the job. If you cannot work with your boss anymore, you can leave knowing you have done everything in your power to please him or her.

32 Career Enemies

Enemy #16: How Your Organization Can Affect Your Career

Employers are supposed to support and encourage their employees. They train, manage, and help them to succeed. However, some employers can cause difficulties for their employees' careers. Knowing how to effectively deal with an employer who stands in the way of your advancement can help you succeed.

1.) Know Your Employer Well – You should know the culture of the institution of your employer inside and out. If it is prone to pay low wages, treat employees poorly, hurt customers if something hurts their bottom line, you need to know about it. The reputation your employer has outside of the walls of its headquarters can impact how seriously a potential future employer will consider your application for a position with a new organization.

2.) The Employer May Keep Employees Down – Rather than offering opportunities for professional growth, some employers may offer minimal and sub-standard training. They may keep qualified employees in low positions for too long. Knowing that you may simply not have room for professional growth with a certain company can help you decide whether to take a job offer from it, or whether you should move if you are already employed there.

3.) Employers May Blacklist – If you do something your company doesn't like, and you quit or are fired, your former

32 Career Enemies

employer may blacklist you. This means that competitors will see you as having a tainted reputation and not as a person that they would hire. Former employee associations may also take to badmouthing you, and word can get around that you left for less-than-optimal reasons.

Know who you are working for, and learn the reputations of potential employers before you sign on with them. Employers typically think of their bottom lines first, and some of them may be known to be downright callous toward employees. Protect yourself by asking around in your industry what the reputation of a particular company is before you apply for or accept any job it offers. Doing so can help you find work with a solid company that takes pride and interest in its employees.

32 Career Enemies

Enemy #17: How Insubordination Can Affect Your Career

Disobeying a direct order from a boss and talking back with a negative attitude are two of the worst things you can do in your career. Insubordination is not taken lightly on the job. By doing things your own way, you demonstrate that you don't have respect for authority, that you believe you are smarter than others, and that you don't work well on a team.

First, insubordination shows your bosses that you don't respect their position. While you should be able to express your opinion without fear of reprisal, there is a line to not cross when it comes to respect for your superiors. A bad attitude from you simply indicates to them that you are a difficult person to work with and that they should not consider you for promotions or special assignments. In fact, insubordination is considered to be rudeness, and you could lose your job over it.

Next, being insubordinate sends a message to your co-workers that you believe you are smarter than they are. There is nothing more irritating than someone on the job who does not consider other people's opinions to be valid. They are bent on doing work their own way, and the general air of "I'm smarter than you" leaves a bad taste in colleagues' mouths. No one wants to be around people who brag, even silently, that they are more intelligent or worthy of an honor.

32 Career Enemies

Finally, since insubordinate people often think they're smarter than others, they don't tend to work well on teams. Collaboration is essential to career success today. If you flat out refuse to work with someone or to take direction from a team leader, you can lose your job, be demoted, or not be considered for future team tasks that could advance your career.

A final thought, insubordination can also endanger you or others. Disobeying a work safety rule just because you think it's not relevant, for example, can cause you or your co-workers physical harm. If you don't think a rule is worth following, ask why it exists, or go through the proper channels to get it changed. If that doesn't work, find another job, but don't risk not getting a good recommendation from your boss when you leave because you were insubordinate.

32 Career Enemies

Enemy #18: How Office Politics Can Affect Your Career

Office politics is not a game you want to play. Getting involved in other people's squabbles and bid for position and power is petty and can negatively affect your career. Politics leads to back-biting, misunderstandings, lies, communication problems, and a generally unproductive work atmosphere. Loyalties are made and broken all the time in offices, and it is best if you remove yourself to avoid being sucked in.

Office politics can distract you from your work to the point that you are turning out poor-quality materials. When your boss notices, he's got reason to fire or demote you, or possibly deny you a promotion. Stay focused on your job. This translates to happier customers and more money for the company. More money for the company often means more money for you.

The making and breaking of alliances in the office can also cause you to make people angry. If you remain neutral in the hubbub, you are less likely to make enemies. Fewer enemies mean more people like you and want to work with you. Fewer personnel personality conflicts ensue, and your employee file stays empty of written reprimands and warnings.

Finally, participating in office politics contributes to a negative work atmosphere. If you stay out of the mess and try to improve the environment with your detachment, people will

32 Career Enemies

notice. You will set an example for others to emulate. This is the sign of a good leader. Your bosses may recognize your efforts and raise you above those vying for a promotion.

Gossiping, maneuvering and otherwise trying to climb on top of people all on their way up the same career ladder is never a good idea. Avoid remarking when people gossip or ask your opinion on controversial topics affecting your company. People will pick up on the fact that you are not interested in participating, and they will likely leave you alone. You will incur more good than ill will from your colleagues, be able to concentrate on your work, and produce good products. Your customers will notice that you are more attentive to their needs than your colleagues as well, adding to the list of people appreciative that you are above office politics.

32 Career Enemies

Enemy #19: How Not Getting Along With Co-Workers Can Affect Your Career

Going to work can actually be enjoyable if you have fun with your co-workers while you're on the clock. You make friends, tell a few jokes, and just enjoy being in each other's company. However, there is always that one person on staff who you have to deal with, not because you want to, but because your job requires it. That person is grumpy, has a bad attitude, and is generally unpleasant to be around. You don't want to be that person at work. No one likes you, and they can make your job miserable in return.

First, not getting along with your co-workers results in isolation. It's one thing if you like working alone, but you don't have to make everyone around you not like you just to have this privilege. If you are a manager and you don't get along with other people, don't expect your employees to come to you when they have a big problem. They will not like working for you and will likely be less productive because of it. Your colleagues won't want to share ideas or learn from you, either. You will be professionally isolated.

Additionally, not getting along with your co-workers reflects poorly on you. You will be known as the person who cannot cooperate, must have her own way, and who instigates/perpetuates arguments. This can result in your being reprimanded on the job and in a poor work record. You could be fired for your inability to work with others, or you may

32 Career Enemies

be demoted or never promoted.

Make an effort to work well with your co-workers. This will likely mean biting your tongue and not speaking when someone makes you mad. You must also learn to let little things, like someone not refilling the paper drawer in the copier, go. There are more important things to get mad about. Finally, when you do have a disagreement about something with a co-worker, approach the person directly in a non-confrontational way. Repeat to the other person what he has said to ensure you heard correctly and to make the other person feel you are taking what he says seriously. Find mutual ground for a solution.

32 Career Enemies

Enemy #20: How Poor Work Performance Can Affect Your Career

If you don't care about your job, who will? Demonstrating that you could care less about your work is likely to result in your being fired, not getting a promotion, or being the first to be laid off when business turns bad. Not only does your poor work make you look bad, but it can make your colleagues and your organization appear less-than-stellar as well.

Work performance can happen for a number of reasons. First, you may simply hate your job. You may have a desire to hurt your company by doing poor work. However, you may also have personal problems outside of work that interfere with your performance on the job. It could also be that you are not good at your job.

If you don't like your job, there is still no reason to not try your best to do good work. When you make it clear you don't care, bosses, customers, and colleagues will notice. They may not want to work with you for fear that their own performance may suffer. You may also be fired or laid off at the first opportunity. When it is time to apply for new jobs, you will probably find that you can't get anyone to write you a letter of recommendation.

When personal problems interfere with your work, the end results will probably be the same: getting fired or laid off. You may also be reprimanded by your boss and have a negative report put in your employee file. People may view you with a

32 Career Enemies

bit more sympathy than if you purposely do poor work, but you will likely still end up jobless or without the opportunity to advance.

Finally, if you are not good at your job, your work quality will obviously suffer. Take the initiative to seek professional training. Approach your boss about getting extra support, mentoring, and training first. If she can't help you, find assistance outside the company. In the end, if you are just not good at your job, accept it, and move on to another position in which your talents will shine.

32 Career Enemies

Enemy #21: How Being a Workaholic Can Affect Your Career

No doubt you want to impress your bosses and perhaps outperform your co-workers. This can lead to awards, recognition, and a higher salary. Working hard to make your superiors happy can even land you a promotion. However, there is a flip side to having a good work ethic that can negatively affect your career. Your work ethic just might be too good.

First, if you are a workaholic, you may find that you are not as productive as you could otherwise be. For example, if you work 80-hour weeks, but you do not sleep much before you go back to work, being tired can cause you to slow down. You may miss important details in your work that you wouldn't if you were getting enough good rest.

Next, your health may suffer. Working too much raises stress levels, which has a host of side effects on your health. It can make you more susceptible to colds and other illnesses. If you have to go to the doctor regularly or take time off from work because you're sick, your work may further suffer. You likely will not be as effective as you could be if you were more relaxed.

Finally, thinking about work all the time can make you difficult to get along with, according to MrCareer.com. When you are anxious, stressed, or depressed, you're not that much fun to

32 Career Enemies

be around. Your colleagues may complain about you to your boss, which would negate any hard working that you've been doing. You may not get the promotion you've been wanting, either.

Obsessing over your work is a mental issue that can actually cause the quality of your health and work relationships to decline. Workaholics need work and personal time limits to help them manage their thoughts about work. It is a good idea to go the extra mile when your company needs you, but to do so all the time can end up backfiring and leave you with disgruntled customers, co-workers, and bosses. Manage your time well, take vacations regularly, and ensure that your health is not compromised by work by getting adequate rest.

32 Career Enemies

Enemy #22: How too much Pride Can Negatively Affect Your Career

As a professional, you should be confident in your work. If you aren't, you appear ineffective and unable to do your job well. However, being too proud of your abilities can also negatively inhibit your career. Check your attitude and your interactions with others before you alienate co-workers and customers. Doing so can help you stop a downward spiral toward demotion or even termination.

First, being to prideful can sometime put make others feel uncomfortable. When you come across as thinking your work is of the best quality and that you are more intelligent than other people, you lose the respect of others. Your co-workers view you as a know-it-all that won't let other people get a word in edgewise during business meetings and who continually puts others down. No one wants to work or hang out with someone who is arrogant.

Additionally, your pride can keep you from learning more. Your colleagues will not want to share their knowledge or insight with you on projects on which you are working. This can limit the quality of your work because you don't have all the useful information you could have to complete it. People will avoid sharing ideas with you because you shut them down when they mention their ideas and then state how much better your ideas are.

32 Career Enemies

Finally, your pride can blind you to the fact that your work may not be as good as it really is. If you are a salesperson, for example, you may find that you lose customers to co-workers just because you come across as cocky and too full of yourself. Your pride keeps you from seeing a situations as they truly are, and sometime end up looking like a fool instead of a knowledgeable professional.

Keep your thoughts to yourself on how great you are when you are at work. Listen to other's ideas and kindly comment on their positive aspects. Disagree respectfully by saying, "I see your point. It's valid. Another way to look at the situation is. . .," or "Have you considered that perhaps. . ." Be willing to give and take, to compromise, when it is time to make decisions in your organization. Consider that you can be an even more effective professional by simply remembering that others can teach you new ideas and skills.

Enemy #23: How Being Resistant to Change Can Affect Your Career

Changes will inevitably come in your job, your company, and your industry. If you cannot roll with the punches, you may find yourself in a situation in which you cannot get a promotion or are without a job. Being able to go with the flow in a work environment is a necessary to performing a job well. Consider how being resistant to change can negatively affect your career before you act rashly.

1.) You miss out on new opportunities if you are resistant to change. Industries change with the development of new ideas and technology. Companies get new leadership with new ideas. You may be left on the back burner if you refuse to embrace the new changes going on around you. For example, you may miss out on important trainings that can help you land a promotion.

2.) You may also negatively affect your professional relationships with colleagues by resisting change. When your colleagues are excited about changes occurring in your organization, for instance, and you constantly complain that you have to adapt, they will no longer wish to be around you. They may distance themselves from you and choose to no longer associate with you.

3.) You could lose your job or be denied a promotion if you don't want to adapt to changes at work. Your boss will see you

32 Career Enemies

as someone who is difficult to work with and who does not possess the capability to envision and embrace the future. This can mean that you will be passed over for a promotion, or, when lay-offs occur, you are the first to be let go. If your resistance is strong enough, you may even be fired.

Having a good attitude about positive changes at work can help you learn about new concepts and equipment that can help you become an expert in your field. It helps you to keep your friends and find new ones. You will be seen as a flexible person who is willing to take risks for the betterment of the company and his own career if you can embrace change.

32 Career Enemies

Enemy #24: How Not Being Appreciative/Grateful Can Affect Your Career

People want to be acknowledged for the good work they do. A simple "thank you" goes a long way to earning the respect of colleagues and subordinates. If you do not make being grateful part of your career, you will turn people away from you who may be able to help you in your career down the road. Most importantly, however, is that not being appreciative can make you feel less than your best.

If you are in a position of authority, the people who work for you want to hear you say that you are thankful for the good work they do. This simple act of kindness is something that everyone likes to hear. It is the cheapest employee motivator. Your employees will view you with respect when you honor their work with appreciation.

You feel better when you are appreciative of others, and they want to be around you. This grows your support network, and you have even more people who care about you. This further increases your feeling of well-being.

Being grateful is also a way to improve your general attitude. When feeling and expressing gratitude, you are less likely to think negative thoughts or complain about your work to others. Smiling becomes easier, and you can better relax. Your stress level decreases, which can improve the quality of your work because you are not in a negative mindset.

32 Career Enemies

The words "thank you" also are important on a more selfish level because they stick in people's minds. If you say you are grateful to someone, she will remember that. When you need a favor in the future, she will likely remember that you are a decent person with good manners. If you need a letter of recommendation, she is more likely to want to help you get that promotion and write you a glowing reference.

Today, try to say thank you to at least one person. Be specific about what you are thankful for. Write a list of other people to thank in the coming days. You will begin to notice a change in how others receive you and how you feel about yourself.

32 Career Enemies

Enemy #25: How Unemployment Can Affect Your Career

While you search for that perfect job and collect unemployment, know that you may be doing your career more harm than good. While being laid off is not your fault, you may find that it is a wiser career move to start working at a job that is not the exact one you want, at least for a little while.

Beyond the obvious fact that working at any job is probably better than collecting small, unemployment checks for your bank accounts, having a job indicates to employers that you are a hard worker, dedicated to providing for yourself and your family. If a future employer asks why you worked retail for 8 months when you want a job as an engineer, simply explain that you needed money to pay the bills, but that you were consistently looking for work in the engineering field.

Not working just shows that you might be too picky. Some employers might interpret your lack of a job history after getting laid off as a sign of laziness. While it makes sense to look for the perfect job for a little while, two years of unemployment is a bit much.

In addition, if you are out of work for a long time, it can indicate to an employer that you don't take the initiative to improve your situation or that of others. They might wonder why you didn't volunteer in your field or take a retraining program to try a new career if you couldn't find a job in the industry you wanted.

Furthermore, if you are unemployed for a significant period of time, you may find that you do not have the experience or training necessary to keep up with changes in your field. If you have not been attending training classes, volunteering, or going to relevant conferences and seminars, it indicates that you are not interested in staying up to date on what is going on in your industry.

Even if you are out of work, the responsibility is on you to prove to employers that you have what it takes to be a good employee. Drive, ambition, a sense of responsibility, and a good work ethic while you are unemployed can help you to become employed.

32 Career Enemies

Enemy #26: How Not Staying Up to Date Can Affect Your Career

Falling out of step with best practices in your industry can leave you behind. You can end up without a raise or promotion, be the first to be laid off, or even be fired. While it takes hard work to learn new methods and technologies and then implement them on the job, the repercussions of not doing so can far outweigh the effort it takes to master them.

First, your colleagues will know more than you about your field. This can mean that they are given special assignments or get promoted faster than you. If you don't know what is going on in your field, don't expect others who do to wait around for you to figure it all out or to reward you for not taking the initiative and learning.

In addition, being behind the learning curve can mean trouble for your career because you may lose prestige and end up with a less-than-stellar reputation among colleagues and customers. People go for advice to those who research innovative ideas, come up with their own ideas, and then have success implementing them. Not being as well-received by colleagues and customers can translate into fewer customers and lower income.

Finally, not learning the latest in your field makes you appear like you're dragging your heels in the mud. You seem to be a cantankerous individual who is not open to new ideas. You

32 Career Enemies

appear to be a know-it-all who really doesn't know much of anything. This negatively affects work relationships. You will be known as someone who is not flexible, who has no energy to try new ideas, and who is happy with the status quo. You will be thought of as the person who is not interested in improving himself or his work.

Attend professional conferences, implement new ideas and products from trade shows, network with other professionals in your field, read trade publications, join professional societies in your field. Take steps to ensure you are a lifetime student. You will be seen as someone who wants to make progress. You will inspire others to try out new ideas as well, and you will be a catalyst in improving procedure and products in your industry.

32 Career Enemies

Enemy #27: How Your Social Media Activities Can Affect Your Career

Remember those pictures taken at the party last weekend, the ones that your friend tagged you in but didn't ask permission to post to Facebook? Those pictures can land you in hot water at your job. Social media can lead to reprimands, demotion, and even termination. On the other hand, social media can help you build your professional reputation if you use it correctly. Care for your social media reputation so that it can help, not hinder, you.

Consider the negative ways social media can affect your career first. It's important to be cautious about it because your boss or potential employers may view your profiles. If employers see a loud-mouthed, immodest, inappropriate individual, they are not likely to want to even call you in for an interview.

Your boss may simply fire you. When you're at parties, put your drink down before your picture is taken. Ask your friends to notify you before they put your pictures online. Tone down your status updates and tweets. No one needs to know the private, personal details of your life, and you don't need to air virulent political, personal, or religious messages. Set your profile to private, or share it just with family with friends to avoid having your employer see anything negative if you need to share personal information, like health updates.

32 Career Enemies

Social media can also enhance your job prospects. A LinkedIn profile, a professional website with your resume and portfolio, and blog postings on industry websites of credible professionals are targeted, smart ways to get employers and your boss to notice your passion about your job and your industry and your desire to learn more. To appear as professional as possible, use professional photos in your profiles, and use proper grammar and punctuation in all of your postings, both professional and personal.

Handle your social media presence with finesse and careful attention. The slightest mistake can create mayhem in your career. A single word taken in the wrong way, or a comment on an article or blog sent in a negative spirit can make or break your professional future. Treat your social media reputation as you would crafting your resume. Choose your formatting and wording carefully to put yourself in the best light.

32 Career Enemies

Enemy #28: How Your Health and Fitness Can Affect Your Career

If you are not in shape, it doesn't mean that your career will suffer, but imagine how being healthier could positively impact your job. Being overweight and eating poorly can cause you to not perform to your potential. This leads to negative effects in your career. By taking care of yourself, you signal that your health is important and that you have your priorities in life straight.

First, if you are significantly overweight or obese, you may have other health concerns, such as high blood pressure. Having a high-stress job compounds your blood pressure problems. You may have to be on medications to reduce it, but you may also find that you have a difficult time keeping your blood pressure under control if you lose your temper at work. Losing your temper can increase your chances of being fired.

Additionally, if you are out of shape, you may get sick more often. This can translate into more trips to the doctor and more time off work. If you use up all -- or more – of your sick days, you may lose your chance at a lucrative promotion or career-advancing assignment. People who are not in shape may also simply visit the doctor more often because they are unhealthy in other areas. For example, you may have diabetes partly as a result of being overweight. This comes with its own complications, like nerve pain and insulin dependence.

32 Career Enemies

Finally, being unhealthy and unfit leads to having less energy. It takes more effort to move your body, and your aches and pains may be more difficult to handle. If you exercise regularly, you will likely sleep better, which leads to more energy during the day. Losing weight diminishes the stress on your joints, which can decrease your pain level as well.

Take time out of your day to exercise. It decreases your stress level, helps you sleep better, reduces blood pressure, and can help you manage chronic diseases. With more energy, you can focus better at work and generally be more productive. This can indicate to your superior that you are dedicated to improving yourself, which can encourage him to think that you would apply yourself as diligently in a new, better-paying position.

32 Career Enemies

Enemy #29: How Choosing the Wrong Career Can Affect Your Career

You may have spent years in school and thousands of dollars on an education to work in a career you hate. You are miserable, your student loans have piled up, and you don't know if you are ever going to enjoy your job. Choosing the wrong career is not the end of the world, although it may feel like it when you wake up every morning to go to work. It can negatively affect your career, though, so before you change careers again, consider your situation carefully.

First, if you choose the wrong career, you simply are unhappy in your work. This can affect your work performance, which, in turn, can affect your chances to get promotions into a new position that you might actually like. Spending eight or more hours a day in a job you don't like can also just make you feel miserable about life in general. You may be short with your colleagues, who may not particularly enjoy being around you. Souring relationships with colleagues is not a good way to get reference letters when you move to a new career.

In addition, you waste a lot of time and money preparing for a job you despise if you choose the wrong career. Loans, time spent in college, and other resources your poured into finding a job on this particular career path are all wasted if you end up doing a job you don't like.

Finally, working in the wrong career wastes valuable time that

32 Career Enemies

you could have spent working in another field gaining expertise. You could have been promoted three or four times in a career field you like if you had not been working in the wrong career field to begin with.

However, remember that it's not too late to start over. Start a new business in the field in which you're interested. Go back to college to learn how to do a new job. Volunteer in the field to get your feet wet to see if you would really like the new career you're thinking about entering. Talk to others in the field to see what their impressions of it are and of your working in it.

32 Career Enemies

Separating your work and personal lives is not always easy. One often seems to bleed into the other, causing problems. When your personal life affects your job, you risk losing it. While it would seem that what you do away from the job site on your own time is your business, it often is not. Your bosses may feel that what you do outside of work reflects badly on them, on the company, or on the industry. As a result, they may choose to reprimand or even fire you.

Take the case of a professional sports player. Initially, his league suspended him for two games after reports of a dispute with a female where a video emerged of him dragging his fiancé – now his wife -- unconscious out of an elevator. When another video was released that showed him punching the same woman twice, his sport's league suspended him indefinitely. At least, one other sport's league said that the player cannot play for them while he is suspended from his current league.

When your negative actions in your personal life become known to your co-workers, you may lose your job and find it hard to retrieve employment again. Your reputation becomes ruined, and if you end up with a criminal record, it will follow you for years. In some cases, a person may have the option to have the charges expunged from their record, but his employer will still know of his pass unethical actions.

If you feel that your personal issues are out of control, consider talking with a counselor or seeking other professional

32 Career Enemies

help. For example, if you come to work inebriated at times, a recovery program could be helpful in getting you back on the right professional and personal track. If you are going through a difficult divorce or perhaps taking care of a sick relative, build and rely on a support network to provide you with the relief you need to come to work ready to do your best. Everyone needs help at some point, and asking for help is the first positive step you can take to saving your job.

32 Career Enemies

Enemy #31: How Using Alcohol and Drugs Can Negatively Affect Your Career

Drugs and alcohol and your job are not a good combination. In fact, they are a lethal trio in more ways than one. It is imperative that you avoid using either one when you are working. You can put yourself, others, and your job at stake if you don't. Consider drugs and alcohol to be the worst refreshments you can have while on the job.

First, drugs and alcohol impair your judgment. You are likely to make rash and illogical decisions while under the influence of either. That might mean that your respond inappropriately to a customer or even that you get behind the wheel of a vehicle and drive while intoxicated or high.

Second, using drugs and alcohol are clearly against the policy of most, if not all, employers. You probably agreed when you started working with your company to avoid using drugs and alcohol while on duty. You would be breaking your word if you ignore the fact that you agreed to this condition of employment and then use drugs or alcohol. Breaking your word shows your employers that you are not to be taken seriously and that you are not a person of integrity.

Finally, and most importantly, if you use drugs or alcohol, you risk endangering your own or someone else's life. Operating machinery or driving a car while intoxicated or high – even slightly so – slows your reaction times and your ability to make decisions to the point where you can cause accidents that

32 Career Enemies

result in serious bodily harm and death. You may also damage or destroy company property or merchandise while driving or operating machinery while you're inebriated or high. You will probably immediately lose your job and have difficulty finding another one. You may also face criminal charges that will haunt your job search for years to come.

The best way to stay out of trouble is to just not use drugs or alcohol, period. If you do, though, be sure you're not drunk or high before you come to work. You'll save your job and maybe even a life.

32 Career Enemies

Enemy #32: How Criminal Activities Can Affect Your Career

Having a criminal record does not necessarily mean that you will not be able to find a good job. However, it does place significant restrictions on the type of work you can do. Many employers are not interested in working with individuals who have broken the law. This can translate into liability issues, damage to the company, or other negative consequences for the companies if they commit crimes again.

First, you may be shut out of your preferred industry or job title. For example if you have a criminal history relating to sex or child abuse, you can forget about working as a teacher or child care worker. Having certain types of crimes on your record will get you barred by law from working in certain industries ever again. This can significantly impact your future earnings by forcing you to work in another field. You may also have to train for a completely new career.

Second, employers may see you as untrustworthy. If you stole from an employer in the past and were convicted of it, it is unlikely that a future employer would want to hire you. You have worked without integrity in the past, and there is not much reason to think that you would change your ways now, in the minds of many employers.

Having a criminal record does not mean, however, that your career is over. You may have to go back to school and find a

32 Career Enemies

new one, but you can begin anew. Employers do take into consideration the seriousness of your past offenses and how long ago they occurred when they consider you for employment. Working hard as a volunteer and developing a working history will help you get a job in a satisfying field.

Many nonprofit organizations help those with criminal records train for new jobs, learn how to do interviews, dress the part of a professional, and find new jobs. They often have agreements with local employers that are willing to hire former criminals. Working hard in one of these organizations' programs can get you off on the right foot to beginning a new career.

32 Career Enemies

About the Author

Clarence Riley has held several positions over the course of a military career and a long career in corporate America. He strongly believes that the time spend in the military after high school was the key to preparing for a professional career.

Over the past 35 years, Clarence spend time in corporate America dedicated to the technology industry. He served several years as a software developer before accepting a managerial position where he remained for the bulk of his time. He is currently serving in corporate America as a Technical Consultant.

With degrees in Computer Science and Business Management, he prepared himself for a Career that will be rewarding and satisfying to his personal and professional life. He is a strong believer that hard work with a positive attitude while always putting God and family first will opening doors that seems impossible at times.

During the course of his career, he personally experienced or observed many of the challenges in this book referred to as Career Enemies. He was inspired to write this book in order to share the knowledge he had gained over his many years in the work force so that others can benefit. Mr. Riley spend time planning and studying on how the material in the book could be presented as a book and used as a reference guide

32 Career Enemies

through-out ones career before publishing the material.

For those entering into the work force, Clarence believes that the information contained in 32 Career Enemies will provide them with knowledge that is not taught in high school or college. For individuals currently starting a new career or looking to advance in their current career, he believes that the information in this book will prepare them for the challenges they may face in the future or challenges they will be able to assist family members or friends with facing. Mr. Riley's web address is www.ClarenceRiley.com.

www.ingramcontent.com/pod-product-compliance
Lightning Source LLC
Chambersburg PA
CBHW070934180526
45168CB00003B/1068